remember, all of those magnificent quilts you now see in museums and antique shops weren't made by artists. They were made by ordinary people just like us. The quilts were intended to sit not in museums but on beds and to keep the family warm. We sometimes can get awfully hung up on perfection and make too many demands upon ourselves. There is a tradition that old-time quilt makers purposely put a mistake in their quilts to prove that only God was perfect. If you find that you've made a terrible "boo-boo," you have your choice: You can either rip it out and start over or leave it and say that you put it there on purpose!

We quilt makers feel that our quilts, like our children, deserve to have names. Sometimes we think of the name before we begin the quilt; sometimes the name comes to us as we are working, and then there are those quilts that remain nameless until the very last stitch has been taken. Then as we pull out the final basting thread, and give the quilt a final shake to get rid of any excess thread and dust, the perfect name settles onto the quilt as if some magic being had known all along what the quilt name should be. Ruth Bell calls this sampler "Old Glories," maybe because it is made up of many old-time quilt blocks. When you have finished your sampler, crown it with a name, sign it, and date it.

Rita Weiss

Rita Weiss
Quilting Director

General Directions

Before starting to work on your sampler wall hanging, carefully read through the general directions.

Choosing the Fabrics

Old-time quilts were traditionally made of 100% cotton, and this is still the fabric most experienced quilt makers prefer. It is easy to work with and will wear much better than almost any other type of fabric. If you have difficulty locating 100% cotton, you can use a blend; a small amount of synthetic fiber combined with cotton may, in fact, make the fabric easier to launder, but try not to use anything with more than approximately 30% synthetic. Fabrics for quilt making should be soft and fairly closely woven so that the seams will hold and the edges will not fray easily when cut. Be careful, however, of fabrics that are so closely woven that you will have difficulty pushing the needle through them. Avoid any fabrics that have been treated with a finish; they are difficult to work with.

Before you begin work on your quilt, be sure to wash your fabric to check that it is colorfast and preshrunk (don't trust those manufacturers' labels). Test for colorfastness by washing in fairly hot water. Be especially careful of reds and dark blues; they have a tendency to bleed if the initial dyeing was not carefully done. Fabrics which continue to bleed after they have been washed several times (try adding some vinegar or salt to the water to set the color) should be eliminated now. No sense in doing all of that work and have

the colors run in the finished quilt. All fabrics should be preshrunk because some fabrics tend to shrink more than others. A quilt made of different fabrics, not preshrunk, could end up in a later washing with puckered seams if one fabric shrinks more than another.

Washing your fabrics will also give you the opportunity to make certain that the fabrics will react the same way when washed. A fabric with a great deal of synthetic may wrinkle differently from a fabric that is 100% cotton, and this difference can turn up to haunt you in your finished quilt. By the way, fabrics that wrinkle too much can present a problem in the finished quilt. So eliminate anything now that you suspect may make you unhappy later. Press all of your fabric carefully to remove wrinkles and crease marks.

If you're intending your sampler to be just a wall hanging, you may question whether all this washing and ironing is necessary. You should get into the habit of washing everything before you begin to work anyway, so you might as well start now. And are you sure you are never going to want to wash that wall hanging? Remember you are following in a great tradition of quilt makers; you are making a family heirloom to hand down to your children and grandchildren. Imagine what's going to happen one hundred years from now when some unsuspecting descendant tries to stick your wall hanging in his ultra-sonic washing machine.

The grain line of the fabric should be checked carefully. Lengthwise threads should be parallel to the selvage and crosswise threads perpendicular to the selvage as in **Fig 2** to insure that the fabric is straight so the pieces will be correctly cut. If a fabric is off-grain, you can straighten it. Pull gently on the true bias in the opposite direction to the off-grain edge **(Fig 3)**. Continue doing this until the crosswise threads are at a right angle to the lengthwise threads.

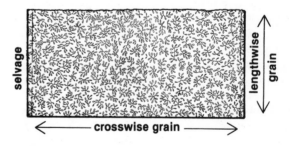

Fig 2

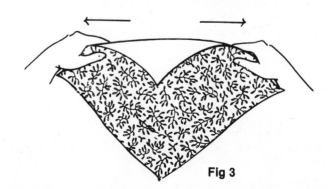

Fig 3

By the way, while we are talking about fabric, a word about thread. Regular sewing thread is used to join the blocks. But if you are using a fabric that is 100% cotton, don't use an all-polyester sewing thread. It will be too strong for your fabric and could actually wear it out over a period of years. Use a 100% cotton thread, or try a cotton-covered polyester. Experiment until you find the right thread. You can piece all of your patchwork blocks with plain white thread, but you will probably want to have matching thread for your applique blocks. You can use "quilting thread" for piecing and applique. Just remember that quilting thread is thicker and seams that cross may become too bulky.

Choosing the Colors

If you like certain color combinations, they are correct for you: Use your own intuitive sense in color choice; be free and creative and don't let anyone (teacher, author, spouse, neighbor) dampen your enthusiasm. If you are looking for ideas for color combinations, look at pictures of quilts or visit museums or quilt shops. If you find a quilt that is especially pleasing to you, try adapting the colors to your own project. Sometimes an idea for a color combination can come from a favorite painting or fabric.

The same quilt blocks done in different color combinations can present a different feeling. Look at the color pictures on the covers of this booklet. You will notice that the sampler on the front cover has been done in a very famous combination of colors; red, white and blue. Now look at the other color versions. The blocks look quite different when they are made in one color family as in the browns, or in two high contrast color families.

Color is such a matter of personal preference that it is difficult to set up any hard and fast rules. Here are some hints rather than rules:

1. In the beginning start with three colors; one dark, one medium and one light. Use one color more than others to give the quilt a sense of unity. This will become the dominant color. Then choose one subordinate color and at least one accent color.

2. Try to use at least one print that contains all of the colors you are planning to use.

3. Do not use prints that are so large that the entire print can not appear in the smallest patchwork piece. Prints of varying size, however, are more interesting than using prints of the same size.

4. You may wish to mix the prints and/or solids in each block, but try to use a combination of light, medium and dark colors in each block. If only two fabrics are required, combine two different values, either light and dark or medium and light rather than medium and medium. Most fabric shops or quilt shops have trained personnel who will be delighted to help you make your color choices. But remember the final choice is yours!!

Cutting the Templates

All of the pattern pieces used in making the quilt blocks in the sampler wall hanging are given in actual-size templates printed on special heavyweight paper in the center of this booklet. If you are planning to make more than one sampler hanging, you may want to make another set of templates. The constant tracing around the template can begin to wear the edges so that by the time you have started to work on your second sampler, the pattern pieces may have changed their shapes.

If you decide that you are going to need additional templates, there are various methods you can use: (1) You can reinforce the original templates by pasting them onto heavier cardboard or sandpaper. (2) You can trace around the original and make one or two sets of duplicates from heavy cardboard, discarding the old templates as they become frayed. (3) You can make a set of permanent plastic templates, either purchasing the plastic sheets at your stationery, craft or quilt shop or using the plastic from household products, such as a coffee can lid or a square fruit juice bottle.

No matter what type of template you decide to use, make sure that your template is completely accurate and that your entire sampler is marked with the same type of template. If you are planning to make duplicates, make them right at the start *before* you start to use your templates. (All of the templates are repeated on the inside of the back cover to aid you if you wish to check the accuracy of your templates once they have been cut.)

The templates for the patchwork blocks are designed to be used for either machine or hand piecing. If you are planning to piece your blocks by machine, cut out the template on the broken line to include the ¼" seam allowance. If you are planning to piece your block by hand, cut out the template on the solid line.

It is important that all templates be cut out carefully because if they are not accurate, the patchwork will not fit together. Use a pair of good-size sharp scissors (not the scissors that you will use to cut your fabric, of course), a single-edged razor blade or an X-Acto knife. Be careful not to bend the corners of triangles.

Cutting the Pieces

Some quilters prefer to mark and cut out all the pieces for an entire project before beginning. Others prefer making one block at a time. This gives them a chance to double-check the pattern and to make certain that they like both the colors and the design. If you make our sampler wall hanging, you may prefer cutting and piecing each block separately, or you may wish to cut out all the pieces at the same time. We recommend cutting and piecing each block separately.

Cutting the pieces is one of the most important steps in making a patchwork block. You must be accurate in order to have the pattern fit smoothly. Start by laying your laundered, freshly-ironed fabric on a smooth surface with the wrong side up. Have all your supplies ready: scissors, rulers, sharp pencils, templates, etc.

Cutting the Patchwork Pieces for Machine Sewing: Lay the cardboard template (cut on the broken line) on the wrong side of the fabric near the top left edge of the material (but not on the selvage), placing it so that as many straight sides of the piece as possible are parallel to the crosswise and lengthwise grain of the fabric **(Fig 4).** Try to keep the long side of the triangles on the true bias by placing the short sides of the triangle on the straight of the fabric. Diamonds should be placed so that two sides of the diamond are on the straight of the fabric (two will be on the bias) as in **Fig 5.** Trace around the template. You can mark

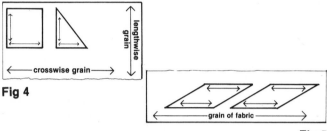

Fig 4

Fig 5

with a regular well-sharpened, hard lead pencil (using a light color for dark fabrics and a regular pencil for light fabrics), but there are some quilt makers who like to use fabric marking pens, ballpoint pens, etc. Test any marking material to make certain that it will not run when wet. There are a number of new cold water soluble quilt marking pens currently on the market. These pens can be used to mark both the back and front of the fabric so you can use them later for marking your quilting design and for marking applique blocks. Cold water is supposed to make these markings disappear, but once again never trust the manufacturer's label. Always test everything just to be sure. Occasionally on a hot summer day, the humidity can cause these markings to disappear. If you live in an area of high humidity, you may just have to work faster on hot days if you want to use these markers. Ruth Bell's favorite marking instrument is the pencil used by architects for drawing on blueprints. These pencils are available at most large stationery stores. They are sold under various brand names, such as Dixon Thinex, white #433 or Eagle Verithin, white #734. Hold your pencil or marker at an angle so that the point is against the side of the template.

Continue moving the template and tracing it on the fabric the required number of times, moving from left to right and always keeping the straight sides parallel with the grain. You will save fabric if you have the pieces share a common cutting line as in **Fig 6,** but if this is confusing, leave a narrow border or margin around each piece.

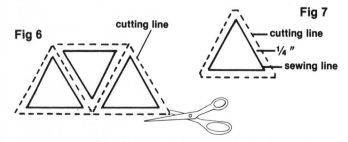

Fig 6

cutting line

Fig 7

cutting line
1/4 "
sewing line

Cutting the Patchwork Pieces for Hand Sewing: Lay the cardboard template (cut on the solid line) on the fabric as described above for machine piecing and trace around it with your marking tool. Now measure 1/4 " around this

shape. Using a ruler, draw this second line. This is the line you will cut on **(Fig 7).** Notice that the first line (where you traced your template) is there to use as a guide for stitching. The seam allowance does not have to be perfect because it will not show. The sewing line, however, must be perfectly straight, or the pieces will not fit together into a perfectly shaped design. After you have had more experience, you may discover that you do not actually need to draw this second line with a ruler; your eye will become so accustomed to the 1/4 " seam allowance that you will be able to detemine it without a ruler.

You also can combine the two techniques when cutting for hand sewing. First trace around the template with the seam allowance to give the cutting line. Then cut the seam allowance off the template and lay this smaller template in the center of the cut fabric piece and trace around it to get the sewing line. This last method is very time consuming and while it will give you an accurate piece, you may become so bored with this double cutting and marking that you never finish your project.

Cutting the Applique Pieces: Place the template on the *right* side of the fabric and then draw around it with your pencil. Now add the 1/4 " seam allowance as for hand sewing the patchwork blocks. The first pencil line is your applique line. As you become more proficient, you may be able to add the additional 1/4 " seam allowance purely by eye, but in the beginning measure around, just to be safe.

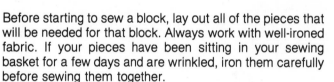

Sewing the Patchwork Block _ _ _ _ _ _ _ _ _

Before starting to sew a block, lay out all of the pieces that will be needed for that block. Always work with well-ironed fabric. If your pieces have been sitting in your sewing basket for a few days and are wrinkled, iron them carefully before sewing them together.

Generally the pieced blocks in this sampler quilt are constructed by joining triangles to make squares **(Fig 8)** and then joining the small squares to make larger squares. Try to join the pieces so that they make horizontal rows **(Fig 9)** rather than "L"s **(Fig 10).** As you fit pieces together, make sure that the corners of adjoining pieces match perfectly.

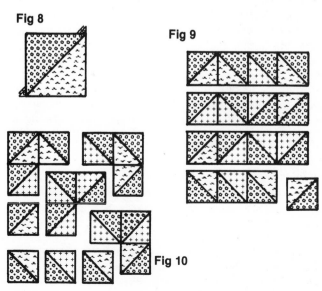

Fig 8

Fig 9

Fig 10

Sewing the Patchwork Block by Hand: Place two pieces together with right sides facing, and place a pin through both pieces at each end of the pencil line **(Fig 11)**. Check on the back to make sure that the pins are exactly on the pencil lines. When sewing large seams, place pins every 1½", removing the pins as you sew past them. Always

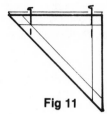

Fig 11

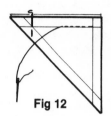

Fig 12

stitch on the sewing line, being careful not to stitch into the margins at the corners **(Fig 12)**. Use a fairly short needle, #7 to #10 (#9 and #10 are the most popular) and no more than an 18" length of thread. Try various needles until you find one which is most comfortable for you. A long needle is not necessary because you should be taking only a few stitches at a time, and a short needle is much easier to work with. Join the pieces with short, simple running stitches **(Fig 13)**, taking a few back stitches. **(Fig 14)** at the beginning and end of each seam rather than a knot. If the seam is very long, it is a good idea to make a few back stitches at various places along the seam. Expert quilt makers try to take 8 to 10 stitches per inch when sewing the patches together. Do not be discouraged if you cannot take such tiny stitches. The important thing is to take small, evenly spaced stitches and to keep the seam as straight as possible along the pencil line. When you sew two bias edges together (as in sewing two triangles along the long side), try to keep the thread taut enough so that the edges do not stretch as you sew them.

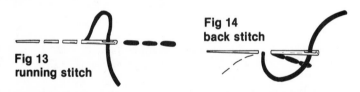

Fig 13 running stitch

Fig 14 back stitch

After you join two pieces together, press the seams flat to one side, not open. Open seams will weaken the quilt. Generally seams can all be pressed in the same direction, but darker pieces should not be pressed so that they fall under the lighter pieces since they may show through when the quilt is completed. You might want to turn the seam on top in one direction, and the seam on the bottom in the opposite direction **(Fig 15)**. This will help to keep seams that are crossed with other seams from bunching at the crossing points. You can clip away excess fabric at these points if necessary. All seams should be ironed before they are crossed with another seam.

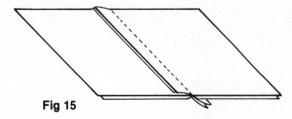

Fig 15

Sewing the Patchwork Block by Sewing Machine: Place the two pieces together with right sides facing. Pieces that are to be machine stitched should be carefully placed so that the top edges of both pieces are even. Set the machine for about 10 stitches to the inch and use a size 14 needle. Machine piecing is best done with the straight stitch foot and throat plate on a machine. Measure ¼" from your needle hole to the right side of the presser foot and place a piece of tape on the plate. Keep the edge of your piece lined up with this marking, and you will be able to sew with a perfect ¼" seam line. Follow the directions for sewing the pieces together by hand; pin the seam, baste (if desired) and sew. Be careful that you do not sew over pins even if your machine permits this. Sewing over pins tends to weaken the seam.

When crossing seams, be especially careful to match seam to seam. One learns to do this fairly accurately while sewing by feeling with the finger. It helps if the lower seam is turned one way and the top seam the other. Sewing machines are not infallible. Some constantly battle to stretch the top fabric. You can learn to win even though the presser foot tries to win a running battle and get ahead of the feed dog.

You can construct the pieces on the machine by using a production line; that is, do not begin and end your thread with each patch, but let the thread run over a continuous chain of patches **(Fig 16)**. When you have made a row of patches, snip them apart; the threads will eventually be anchored by the cross seams.

Fig 16

After you have joined the pieces, press the seams as described for hand sewing.

Sewing the Applique Block _ _ _ _ _ _ _

The seam allowance must be turned under on each piece of applique along the pencil line, and there are two methods you might want to try. (1) Turn down the seam allowance and finger press the turned-down edges in place. Baste the edges as you turn them, keeping your finger pressing about an inch ahead of the needle. All curved edges should be clipped to keep the outline of the designs; clip all curves to within four or five threads of the penciled line. By the way, since you are going to want to remove all of the basting threads, be sure that you have your knots on *top* of the patches, and use white thread so that the basting will be easy to see. (2) Place the applique shape on the ironing board, wrong side up. Now put the template, which was used to cut the shape, in the center of the piece, inside the seam allowance. Iron the seam allowance portion over the template. Remove the template and iron again. Try to keep the iron away from the edges because this may tend to stretch the shape. Remember to clip all curved edges before pressing under the seam allowance.

After you have turned under the seam allowance on all of the pieces, cut a block of the appropriate background fabric to be used as a base for your applique block. Always cut this square larger than the finished block. Applique sometimes has the habit of causing the fabric to pucker, and you could end up with a square that is smaller than the other squares in your quilt. For our sampler, cut your applique squares approximately 9″ x 9″ **(Fig 17a)**. Now fold the square in half **(Fig 17b)** and then in half again **(Fig 17c)** and iron this fold into the fabric. Open the block and fold diagonally **(Fig 17d)** and iron in the creases. This will give you a number of guide lines and will locate the center of the block **(Fig 17e)**. After you have appliqued the entire block, remeasure the block from the center and cut if necessary, to make the block the required 8½″ x 8½″. Arrange the pieces on the background fabric and pin in place securely. If there are shapes to be overlapped, complete the shapes underneath first so that there is a neat, unbroken line at the top.

Fig 17

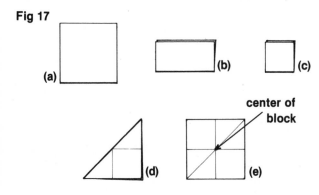

Permanently attach the pieces to the background fabric with a stitch of your own choice. The traditional blind stitch, worked with matching thread is an easy stitch to do, and the stiches "disappear," making it seem as if the patch and the background are one. Another very popular technique is to go around the edges, by machine or hand, using various embroidery stitches (or even a simple running stitch worked with a contrasting thread about ⅛″ inside the edge of the applique piece). The embroidery thread used for the stitching, usually a floss, becomes itself a decorative part of the applique. If you are planning to attach your applique pieces by using your zigzag sewing machine, you do not have to add any seam allowance since the sewing machine embroidery will not only firmly attach the piece but will provide a decorative edge that will prevent the fabric from fraying.

After you have finished appliquing all of the pieces, remove the basting threads and carefully iron the block, taking special pains not to stretch the edges of the appliqued pieces. As a general rule, appliqued blocks do not need to be ironed as flat as patchwork blocks.

Sewing the Pieced and Appliqued Blocks

Two of the blocks in this sampler (the "Six-Pointed Star" and "Grandmother's Flower Garden") combine the techniques of patchwork (or piecing) and applique. Follow the specific instructions with the block, but in general, cut and join the pieces as if they were patchwork, and then sew them to the block as if they were applique.

Blocking the Block

The term "blocking" means keeping the edges straight on all sides of the quilt so that it will be a perfect rectangle when finished. The term applies to the quilt's parts as well as to the entire quilt so the blocking process is a continuous one from start to finish. It will help the blocking process if you have cut all of your patchwork pieces with the straight sides of the pattern parallel to the grain of the fabric because pieces cut on the bias do have a tendency to pucker and stretch.

Place the completed block on your ironing board and measure the sides. All of the blocks in the Old Glories Sampler, for example, should be a perfect 8½″ square (the finished block will actually be an 8″ square; the extra ¼″ all around being the seam allowance that will be used when joining the blocks). By the way, if a block is slightly smaller or larger, don't be concerned. The measurements given with quilt blocks are strictly mathematical; they do not allow for variations which can occur as you work with different fabrics. You can often stretch or shrink the blocks to size during the blocking process. The important thing is that all of the blocks are the same size and perfectly square. Place the block on the ironing board and pull the edges of the block straight with your fingers. Making sure that the block is perfectly square, place pins at the corners and at several places along the edges to hold the block rigidly in place. Cover the block with a damp cloth and steam with a warm iron (or use a steam iron). Do not let the pressing cloth get dry. Iron the edges until they are perfectly square and of equal measurements. The center is ironed last. The block should be ironed perfectly flat with no pucker.

Framing the Block

After you have carefully ironed each block measure the sides. Hopefully the Old Glories blocks will now be 8½″ x 8½″, but again, if they are not, don't be concerned. Simply plan your framing for smaller or larger blocks.

For our sampler, cut two strips of fabric 8½″ (or length of one side) by 1½″. Cut two more strips 10½″ by 1½″. Frame the block as in **Fig 18**, allowing a ¼″ seam allowance all around. Carefully iron the block again, making sure that it is perfectly square. In this manner, frame all of the quilt blocks. Again press your seams to one side—not open.

Fig 18

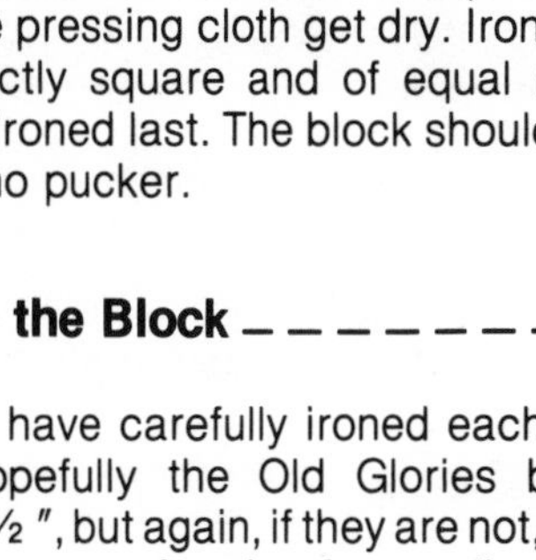

Adding Sashing or Lattice

Often quilt blocks are set without any division between the blocks, creating an optical illusion. Therefore, the design on the completed quilt top seems to bear no relationship to the design of the individual block. The "Road to Oklahoma" block is a good example of this. When used continuously to make a complete quilt, the dark red print squares make a continuous path (road) across the quilt.

A quilt, like our sampler, with many different patterns, always looks better when set apart with strips called "sashing" or "lattice," and we have used sashing with our Old Glories Sampler.

Again begin by measuring your completed blocks. If some of the blocks are slightly smaller than required size, you can stretch them slightly; if they are larger, you can ease the blocks to the sashing as you join them.

To join the Old Glories quilt blocks to the sashing, work as follows:

1. Begin by cutting nine strips which are 10½ " (or size of your block) × 3½ ".

2. Join the first sashing strip to the bottom of the "Grandmother's Flower Garden" block, and to the top of the "Rail Fence" block.

3. Join the second sashing strip to the bottom of the "Rail Fence" block and to the top of the "Desert Rose" block.

4. Join the third sashing strip to the bottom of the "Desert Rose" block and the top of the "Flock of Geese" block.

5. Continue joining the sashing strips to the tops and bottoms of the blocks, following the order in **Fig 19.**

Fig 19

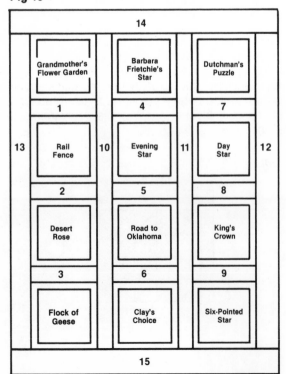

6. You now have three strips which should measure 49½ " including the ¼ " seam allowance at the top and bottom. Again do not be concerned if your measurements are slightly less or more. The important thing is that all three strips must be equal. If they are not, you will once again have to "ease" or "stretch" as you join the sashing.

7. Now cut two sashing strips, each 49½ " × 3½ ". Attach these two strips (Nos. 10 and 11) on either side of the center row of blocks as shown in **Fig 19.** Now attach the first and third row of blocks to the strips. Do this very carefully so that all of the blocks line up. Again, carefully press all seams to one side before joining the next seam.

Adding the Borders

Just as most pictures look better framed, most quilts look best with borders. To add borders to the Old Glories Sampler begin by cutting two more strips which are 49½ " × 3½ " (or the length that you cut your three long sashing strips). These two strips should be attached to the right and left sides of the quilt top in the same manner as you attached the two vertical sashing strips (Nos. 12 and 13). Now carefully measure your quilt at the top and bottom; the Old Glories should measure 42½ ". Cut two additional strips which are 42½ " x 3½ ", and attach these borders (Nos. 14 and 15) to the top and bottom as indicated in **Fig 19.**

If you do not have enough fabric for these long strips you may have to piece them. These pieced seams will be hardly noticeable in the finished quilt, but be sure to iron the seams before joining the strips. Some quilters prefer tearing the long strips, but tear only horizontally—never vertically. First cut off the selvage edge, measure 3½ " and tear carefully. Always be sure to iron very carefully those strips which have been torn before you use them, as tearing has a tendency to pull the fabric off grain.

Your quilt top will need a final blocking. Follow the instructions for blocking the individual blocks. If you find it difficult to work on the ironing board now, you might try your dining room table or the living room floor. If you have been careful with the ironing of each individual block, you shouldn't need much ironing and blocking at this point. Your top is now ready for the quilting.

Preparing the Quilt Top

A completed wall hanging or a completed quilt consists of three parts: the top, the filler or batting, and the backing. Quilting stitches are used to hold the top to both the backing and the batting. Choose the best possible materials for your backing and your batting if you want your quilt to last. Besides, all of your beautiful work deserves the best!

There are a number of different types of batting on the market. Because it was the only kind available, antique quilts, with very ornate quilting designs, were always made with a very thin batting (there's no way that a quilter could have made all of those fancy curlicues through thick batting). This traditional, thin batting is still available. Thinner batting, however, requires more quilting stitches to hold it to the top and backing; antique quilts usually have their quilting lines no more than 1″ apart. Very thick batting is usually used for tied quilts only, since pushing a quilting needle through all of that thickness would be almost impossible. For a first quilting project, buy a medium weight (¼″ to ½″ thick) bonded polyester sheet batting. It will be the easiest to work with, and it won't shred, lump or pull. You'll be able to do almost as much or as little quilting as you wish without fear of the batting slipping around when the quilt is washed. Don't buy polyester *stuffing,* which is intended for pillows or toys. Sheet batting is made especially for quilts; it is "bonded" into a flat sheet and then rolled up for ease in handling.

Many old-time quilt makers used unbleached muslin for their quilt backings, but most modern quilters prefer a color that harmonizes with the quilt top. Some fabric and quilt stores sell extra wide-width fabric to use as quilt backing. Most quilt tops, however, will be wider than the available fabric, and you will have to sew lengths together to make the necessary widths. If you are joining fabric, don't have a seam down the center. Cut off selvages and make a center strip that is about 36″ wide and have narrower strips at the sides. Seam the pieces together carefully and iron seam open. (This is the only time in making a quilt that a seam should be pressed open!) Make certain that whatever fabric you decide to use for the quilt backing is soft and loosely woven so that the quilting needle can pass through evenly. Sheets are usually not good backing material since they tend to be closely woven, and this can present a problem in the quilting.

Before the completed quilt top is joined to the batting and backing, you may want to mark the quilting pattern on it. For our Old Glories Sampler, follow the suggested quilting pattern in **Fig 26** or use your own design. Quilting which is done inside the blocks need not be marked since you are quilting around the patchwork and the applique. You may however, want to mark other quilting motifs, such as the design on the sashing and borders of the Old Glories. A quilting template, such as the one provided here, is often used for this. Mark all of the quilting lines on the *right* side of the fabric. There are a number of methods for marking the design on the fabric. You might want to test these to make certain that they will wash out if necessary. One of the easiest methods is to use a hard lead pencil, or if the fabric is dark, chalk or a piece of white soap trimmed to a thin point. If you sew directly on the pencil or chalk lines, they probably will not show when the work is finished. You might also want to experiment with some of the water-soluble marking pens or the architect's pencils discussed earlier. The best advice is to test all of these marking materials first to find the one that works best for you.

Lay your neatly ironed and marked top on a large flat surface (the living room floor or a large dining room table) and measure your completed top. If all of your measurements have been exact, our Old Glories will measure 42½″ × 55½″ (the extra ¼″ all around being the seam allowance that will be used in the final binding of the quilt).

Cut your batting and your backing according to the *actual* size of the quilt top, making them approximately 2″ larger

on all sides. This is a good practice for a number of reasons. First, if you do your quilting in a frame, this extension can be used to attach the quilt to the frame without damaging the quilt top. Then it's easier—especially for a first project—to get the top centered when you don't have to worry about an exact center. If you are going to use a package of batting designed for a crib quilt (45″ × 60″), use this batting as is. Cut your backing to match the size of your batting.

Carefully place the backing, wrong side up, on a flat surface. To keep the corners from moving, you might want to secure them with thumbtacks, pins, or masking tape. Now unroll the batting and spread it evenly over the backing **(Fig. 20)**. Be sure that there are no lumps and no thin spots which will make your quilting uneven. When you start to work on large quilting projects, you may have occasion to piece the batting. If this is necessary, butt the pieces and join them with wide cross stitches. Don't ever overlap the pieces or stretch batting to fit. This will cause the batting to tear and may make some sections thinner than others. When you are certain that both layers are smooth, pin them together. Then, fasten the batting to the backing with long basting stitches. Start in the center and sew toward the edge with large basting stitches in a number of diagonal lines **(Fig 21)**. If you wish, add additional basting stitches around the edges. Again, put the knots on the outside and use a thread color which will be easy to detect when you are ready to remove the basting

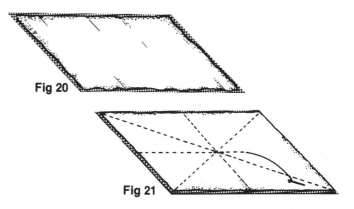

Fig 20

Fig 21

threads. Now lay the quilt top in place over the backing and the batting; line up the center of the quilt top with the center of the batting and the backing. Don't forget that you will have about 2″ of batting and backing extending beyond the quilt top. When you are satisfied that the quilt top is in position, pin it in place and again baste the three layers as you basted the first two **(Fig 22)**. Try to make sure that your basting stitches are no more than 6″ apart.

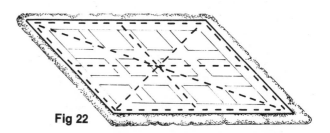

Fig 22

Most old-time quilting was done in a quilting frame, which looks a little bit like a large picnic table without a top **(Fig 23)**. It has two long, removable sides covered with fabric. The quilt is attached to the sides and then rolled around until the center of the quilt (or the spot you are working on) is taut. You begin by working in the center, and as you work, the quilt is rolled to one side or the other exposing the unquilted section. There is nothing that will hold a quilt as well, permitting you to work without worrying about puckers or slips. If you are fortunate enough to own or have access to a quilting frame, by all means use it. We're not going to explain in great detail how to use a frame since the frame itself will come with very specific instructions. However, a quilting frame is a large piece of equipment, and many of us just don't have the room for something that large.

Our sampler quilt, as well as many other quilting projects, can be quilted quite satisfactorily in a quilting hoop **(Fig 24)**. A quilting hoop is made like an embroidery hoop but is larger and sturdier. Quilting hoops are obtainable in needlework and fabric departments and stores as well as through mail order. The hoop can be moved around, and since many come with detachable legs, can be used either on the floor or in the lap.

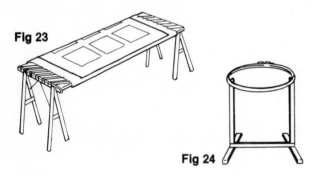

Fig 23

Fig 24

Begin by placing the hoop over the middle of the quilt. Pull the quilt taut, and move the extra fullness toward the edges. Begin to work in the center and quilt toward the outer edges. The quilting stitch has a tendency to push the batting, and by quilting from the center out, you can gradually ease any excess fullness toward the edges rather than finding a big lump in the center of the quilt.

Quilting the Top

The actual quilting stitch is really a fairly simple one for anyone who has ever sewn. There are many books which attempt to teach the quilter how to make the proper stitch. It's something like teaching someone to swim with a swimming manual. You're never really going to learn unless you dive right into the water! The stitch is just the very simple running stitch; the same one you used to join the patchwork pieces if you did them by hand. Getting that running stitch through three thicknesses, however, means that you are going to have to do the stitch a little differently. Instead of just horizontally pushing the needle through the fabric and then pulling it out in one motion, you will probably have to push it vertically all the way through the three layers on one side and then push it back in what amounts to two separate motions. If you are unsure of yourself, you might want to practice on some batting sandwiched between two pieces of fabric and placed in an embroidery hoop.

Use one of the short, fine needles especially designed for quilting (they are called ''betweens''). Try various sizes until you find the one that you like the best. Try to use the shortest possible because shorter needles will mean shorter stitches.

If you quilt continuously for several hours, your fingers may become very sore. Old-time quilters, in fact, used to soak their fingers in hot alum water to toughen the membranes. Today quilters use many techniques for protecting their fingers, but they all wear thimbles! If you have never used a thimble before, you are going to have to now so that you might just as well practice until you are used to it. The thimble is worn on the middle finger of your right hand (or on your left, if you are left-handed); you may want to protect the fingers on your left hand with some tape. By the way, if you should prick your finger as you are working and bleed on your quilt, immediately dab the stain with some cold water. (There's also a theory among quilters that one's own saliva will dissolve a blood stain even quicker than cold water because of the compatibility of our own body fluids.) Blood that has been allowed to dry can remain forever.

Quilting should be done with 100% cotton quilting thread. Once again, if you have made your quilt top of 100% cotton fabric (or fabrics which are mostly cotton) a polyester thread will be too strong. At some point the fabric could conceivably pull away from the thread, and you could end up with tatters and a row of quilting. Quilting thread is strong and usually has a lustrous finish. In addition, it is designed not to knot as easily as other threads. If you are unable to locate 100% cotton quilting thread, you can use a strong (#50 or #30) mercerized cotton or cotton-coated polyester. All quilting threads should be waxed by running them through a cake of beeswax before you start to quilt. This helps to keep your thread from tangling and makes the sewing go more smoothly. Traditionally only white thread was used for quilting, probably because old-time dyes tended to weaken threads. White is still the favorite color of quilters, and although quilting thread is now available in many other colors, most quilters choose white. For your first attempts at quilting, use a white quilting thread because stitches in other colors *will* stand out. White stitching on our red sashing does not stand out as much as red stitching on white would. Once you become extremely sure of your ability as a quilter, and you really want your expert quilting stitches to be seen, feel free to use any color quilting thread you desire.

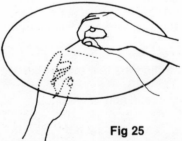

Fig 25

Begin with an 18″ piece of quilting thread with a knot in one end. Go into the quilt through the top approximately ½″ from where you are planning to begin your quilting, and bring your needle up to the quilting line. Pull gently but firmly and the knot will slip through the top layer into the padding where it will not be seen. Place left hand under the spot where the needle should come through. With the right hand push the needle vertically downward through the layers of the quilt until it touches the left hand **(Fig 25)**.

For your first attempts, pull the needle and thread through with the left hand and push the needle back upward to where it is received by the right hand close to the first stitch. As you become more proficient, you will be able to do the entire operation with one hand, merely using the left hand to signal that the needle has penetrated the three layers. Some very experienced quilters are able to put two or three stitches on the needle just as if they were sewing. Try to make the stitches as close together as you can; this is the real secret of fine quilting. Expert quilters insist that quilting stitches should be no less than five to ten per inch. Don't be discouraged, however, if your stitches are longer. It is probably more important that the stitches be evenly spaced and that they are the same length on the front as the back. Don't quilt over the basting stitches; they will become impossible to remove. To finish off a thread, make a single back stitch and run the thread through the padding. Cut. The end will be lost!

If you quilt your Old Glories Sampler by following the quilting plan in **Fig 26,** you will notice that you are quilting ¼″ inside the seam of several chosen squares and triangles in the patchwork blocks. Those not quilted now stand out prominently. The applique blocks are quilted ⅛″ around the figures. For an even more attractive look, you can also "echo" quilt around the applique pieces; that is, quilt another line ¼″ beyond the original quilting line. Notice that the quilting template has been used to mark the quilting along the sashing and the borders.

When the entire quilt has been quilted, lift the quilt from the frame or hoop and remove the basting stitches.

Fig 26   suggested quilting lines

Attaching a Binding

Carefully trim the backing and the batting ½″ beyond the edge of the quilt top. From the same fabric you used for the sashing and borders, cut two 2″ strips the length of your quilt (for the sides). Right sides together sew one side strip to one side of the quilt with a ¼″ seam allowance (seam allowance should be measured from the outer edge of the quilt top fabric, not the outer edge of the batting/backing, **(Fig 27).** Turn the binding to the back and turn under ¼″ on the raw edge; slip stitch to the backing **(Fig 28).** Do the other side in the same manner. Then, carefully measure and cut two 2″ binding strips for the top and bottom, and attach in the same manner as the sides. Lightly steam top, bottom and side bindings. If you have worked accurately, a ¾″ binding strip will be showing all around the quilt.

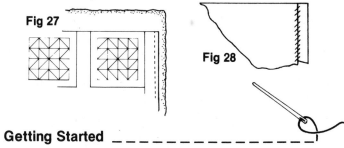

Fig 27

Fig 28

Getting Started

Now it's time to begin your sampler quilt. Here is a list of materials that you will need to recreate the Old Glories Sampler:

⅓ yard of each of the following prints:
    Fabric II,
    Fabric III,
    Fabric IV,
    Fabric V,
    Fabric VII (for patches and applique)
    Fabric VI (for patches and background fabric for appliqued blocks)

2 yards Fabric I (for patches, sashing, borders and binding)

⅔ yard Fabric IX (for framing)

1½ yards Fabric VIII (for one patch and backing)

45″ × 60″ batting (crib size; often called "Baby Batt")

1 pair fabric shears (for cutting fabric)

1 pair sharp scissors, single-edged razor, or X-acto knife (for cutting templates)

Sewing thread	Straight pins
Quilting thread	Sewing needles
Beeswax	Quilting needles
Thimble	Quilting hoop or frame

Sharp pencils, quilting pens, etc. (to mark fabric)

COLOR KEY

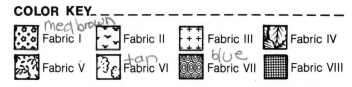

Fabric I (med brown)	Fabric II	Fabric III	Fabric IV
Fabric V	Fabric VI (tan)	Fabric VII (blue)	Fabric VIII

We have made every effort to ensure the accuracy and completeness of these instructions. We cannot, however, be responsible for human error, typographical mistakes, or variations in individual work.

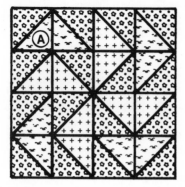

Fig 29

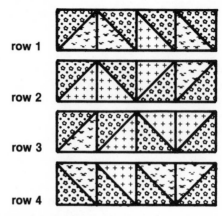

row 1

row 2

row 3

row 4   Fig 30

Dutchman's Puzzle

Old-time quilt makers loved to use the word "puzzle" in naming their quilt blocks. The only "puzzle" here seems to be in arranging the small squares produced by sewing together the triangles. Just follow the diagrams and the "puzzle" will be solved.

Cut the following pieces:

Template A	16 Fabric I
Template A	8 Fabric II
Template A	8 Fabric III

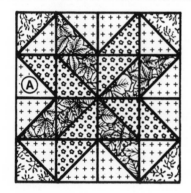

Fig 31

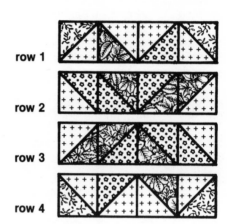

row 1

row 2

row 3

row 4   Fig 32

Barbara Frietchie's Star

Barbara Frietchie's patriotic deed may have inspired John Greenleaf Whittier to write, "'Shoot if you must this old gray head, But spare your country's flag,' she said," but it also inspired a quilter to name her block after this heroine. There is also the tradition that a quilt with this design adorned Barbara Frietchie's bed. A star is often a complicated block to piece, but this version, made of triangles, is easy.

Cut the following pieces:

Template A	8 Fabric I
Template A	12 Fabric III
Template A	8 Fabric IV
Template A	4 Fabric V

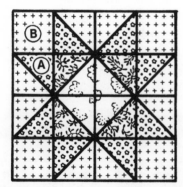

Fig 33

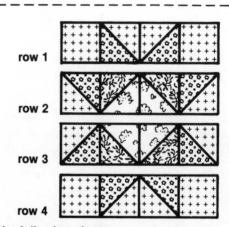

row 1

row 2

row 3

row 4   Fig 34

Evening Star

Undisturbed by pollution or the glare of street lamps, the evening star was certainly a memorable sight to the frontierswoman. It obviously made such an impression that she named her quilt block for this natural phenomena. The block uses both triangles and squares to form this eight-pointed star.

Cut the following pieces:

Template B	4 Fabric III
Template A	8 Fabric I
Template A	8 Fabric III
Template A	4 Fabric V
Template A	4 Fabric VI

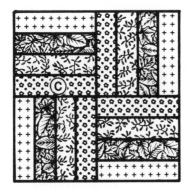

Fig 35

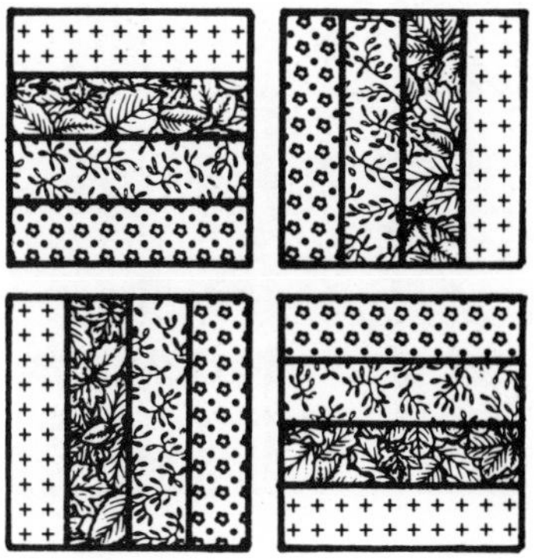

Fig 36

Rail Fence

It is certainly not difficult to see the rails of a fence in this block, and the block is one of the easiest to piece. The only possible problem might arise in placing the "rails" in the right order. Notice that the block actually consists of four squares; each square is made up of four rails. Follow **Fig 36** carefully.

Cut the following pieces:

Template C . . . . 4 Fabric I
Template C . . . . 4 Fabric III
Template C . . . . 4 Fabric IV
Template C . . . . 4 Fabric V

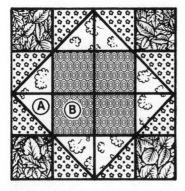

Fig 37

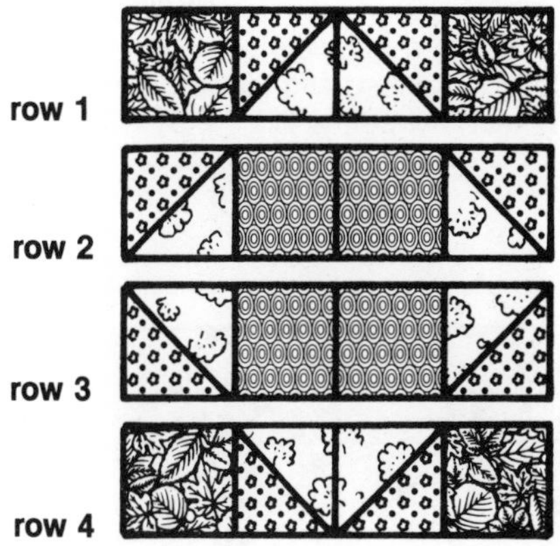

row 1

row 2

row 3

row 4   Fig 38

King's Crown

While this block may not be intended to crown the head of a king, the quilter who first named it may have felt that this quilt block was her "crowning" achievement. The name may very well have come from the bible, the source of many quilt names containing crowns, such as "Crown of Thorns," "Cross and Crown" and "King David's Crown." Since religion was such an important part of the lives of early quilters, many quilt block names derive from the Bible.

Cut the following pieces:

Template A . . . . 8 Fabric I
Template A . . . . 8 Fabric VI
Template B . . . . 4 Fabric IV
Template B . . . . 4 Fabric VII

Fig 39

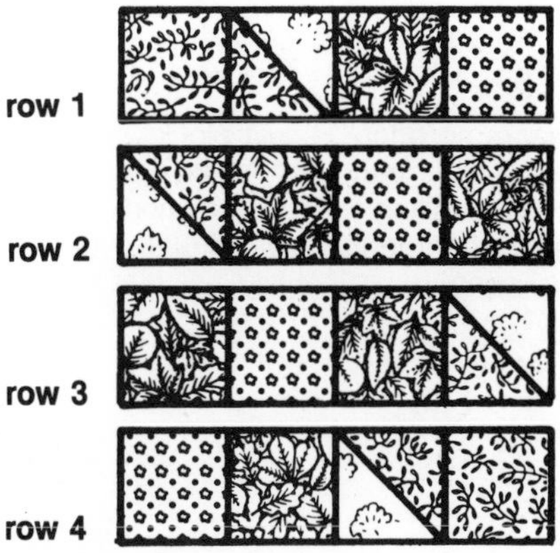

row 1

row 2

row 3

row 4   Fig 40

Road to Oklahoma

The word "road" appears often in quilt names ("Road to California," "Rocky Road to Kansas," "Rocky Mountain Road") perhaps in honor of the journeys early quilt makers took to reach their new homes on the frontier. When done in fewer colors, this block is often called "Jacob's Ladder."

Cut the following pieces:

Template A . . . . 4 Fabric V
Template A . . . . 4 Fabric VI
Template B . . . . 4 Fabric I
Template B . . . . 6 Fabric IV
Template B . . . . 2 Fabric V

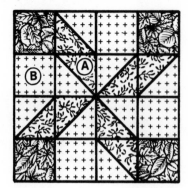

Fig 41

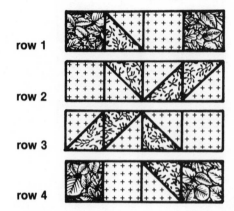

row 1

row 2

row 3

row 4

Fig 42

Clay's Choice

Despite her inabilty to vote, the nineteenth century quilter was well aware of the political scene, and a number of early quilt blocks bear political titles, such as "Fifty-four Forty or Fight," "Tippecanoe and Tyler Too" as well as this one named for Henry Clay. Later the block became "Henry of the West" and finally Clay was completely forgotten when the block became "Star of the West." There is also a tradition that Henry Clay was once asked to judge a quilt contest, and that a quilt made with this design was the winner; hence the title, "Clay's Choice."

Cut the following pieces:

Template A	. . . .	8 Fabric VI
Template A	. . . .	8 Fabric III
Template B	. . . .	4 Fabric IV
Template B	. . . .	4 Fabric III

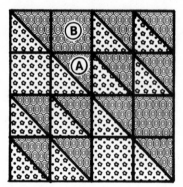

Fig 43

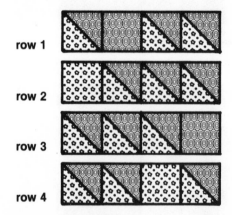

row 1

row 2

row 3

row 4

Fig 44

Flock of Geese

The triangle appears so often in quilt blocks with bird names ("Hovering Hawk," "Birds in the Air," "Wild Goose Chase") that it may be said that the triangle is a bird symbol, one of the few emblematic shapes in American folk crafts. Notice how the stylized bird forms seem to project an illusion of a flock of birds moving in the air.

Cut the following pieces:

Template A	. . . .	12 Fabric I
Template A	. . . .	12 Fabric VII
Template B	. . . .	2 Fabric I
Template B	. . . .	2 Fabric VII

These two blocks are pieced first and then appliqued onto the background. Cut and assemble the pieces as if the blocks were patchwork, marking them on the *back* of the fabric.

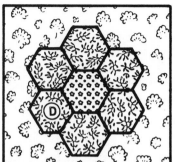

Fig 45

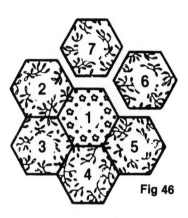

Fig 46

Grandmother's Flower Garden

This is probably America's most popular quilt pattern even though it is not the easiest. Often an entire quilt is produced with endless little hexagons, sometimes several thousand. It is often called "Mosaic," "Honeycomb" or even "French Bouquet." Join the seven hexagons to each other working from the inside out, as in **Fig 46.** Baste the seam allowance back along the outer edges following the general instructions for applique. Find the exact center of the pieced applique. Pin in place and then applique the pieced "Grandmother's Flower Garden" to the background block.

Cut the following pieces:

Template D	6 Fabric V
Template D	1 Fabric I
One 9″ × 9″ block	Fabric VI

Fig 47

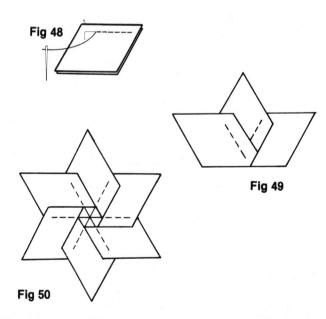

Fig 48

Fig 49

Fig 50

Six-Pointed Star

Although not as popular among quilt makers as the eight-pointed star, used in such quilt blocks as "Barbara Frietchie's Star" or "Evening Star," many blocks (such as "Hexagonal Star" and "Rising Star") are based upon the six-pointed star. This block may be more difficult than the other patchwork blocks in the sampler, but if you work carefully, the construction of a six-pointed star should present no problem. Be sure to cut the six diamonds according to the special instructions for cutting diamonds. Place two diamonds together, making sure that the seams match. Join them; do not sew into the seam allowance **(Fig 48).** Press the seam to one side. Now take the third diamond and join it to the second diamond, making sure that the stitching starts in the same hole as the first stitch in the previous seam. Press the seams flat in the same direction and clip the points **(Fig 49).** Now lay these three diamonds aside and contruct the other half of the star in the same manner.

Place both halves together, exactly aligning the two centers. Stitch the seam; do not stitch through the seam allowances at the center, but let the needle go through the exact tip of each diamond. Press all of the seams flat in a clockwise direction **(Fig 50).**

Press under and baste the ¼″ seam allowance of the outer edge of the completed star. Find the exact center of the background block and match it to the exact center of the appliqued star. Pin in place and applique the pieced "Six-Pointed Star" to the background.

Cut the following pieces:

Template E	1 Fabric I
Template E	1 Fabric II
Template E	1 Fabric III
Template E	1 Fabric IV
Template E	1 Fabric V
Template E	1 Fabric VII
One 9″ × 9″ Block	Fabric VI

These two blocks are completely appliqued.

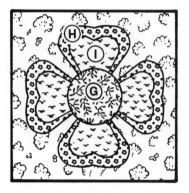

Fig 51

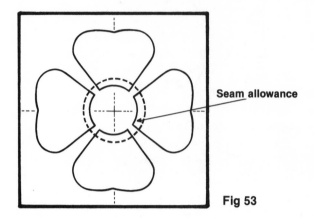

Seam allowance

Fig 53

Desert Rose

Quilt blocks traditionally change names as they change locales: "Maple Leaf" becomes "Cactus Flower"; the "Peony" moves to Kansas where it becomes the "Sunflower," and "Burgoyne Surrounded," made to commemorate Burgoyne's defeat in the American revolution, eventually winds up in northern Ohio as "Road to California." Some quilters call this block "Prairie Rose." It probably depends upon where you see roses, the desert or the prairie.

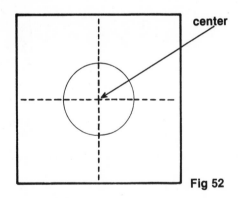

center

Fig 52

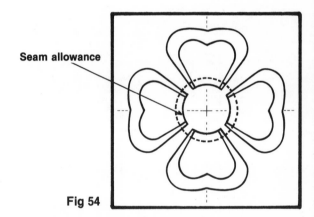

Seam allowance

Fig 54

1. Fold the background fabric in half and then in half again to find the center.
2. Lay Template G on the background fabric, matching centers, and trace around with a pencil (or similar marking tool) to indicate the spot for the circle. **(Fig 52)**.
3. Prepare the large petals, made from Template H, and applique them into position. Note that the bottom seam allowance **(Fig 53)** is left raw.
4. Prepare the small petals, made from Template I, and applique them into position **(Fig 54).** Note that the bottom seam allowance is left raw.

5. Now, fold under the seam allowance around the circle, made from Template G, clipping where necessary to keep the rounded shape. Applique this circle in position covering the raw edges of the petals as in **Fig 51**.
6. Remeasure the block and cut it so that it is exactly 8½ " × 8½ ", keeping the center in its same position.

Cut the following pieces:

Template H . . . . 4 Fabric I
Template I . . . . 4 Fabric II
Template G . . . . 1 Fabric V
One 9" × 9" Block . . . . 1 Fabric VI

Fig 55

Day Star

After you have been making quilts for a long time, the desire to create your own block becomes quite strong. You get the feeling that you want to join that long line of frontierswomen who, often denied any other chance for artistic expression, found a way to express their creativity in designing an intricate quilt block.

This block is Ruth Bell's own creation; she calls it the Day Star.

1. Fold the background fabric in half and then in half again to find the center.

2. Lay Template J on the background fabric, matching centers, and trace around with a pencil (or similar marking tool) to indicate the spot for the circle **(Fig 56)**.

3. Now further divide the block into the spokes of a clock, as in **Fig 57**.

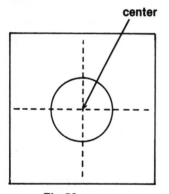

Fig 56   **Fig 57**

4. Prepare six of the petals, made from Template F, and baste them into position on the uneven numbers of the clock **(Fig 58)**. Note that the bottom seam allowance is left raw.

5. Prepare six more petals, made from Template F, and baste them in position on the even numbers of the clock **(Fig 59)**. Note the bottom seam allowance is left raw.

6. Fold under the seam allowance around the circle, made from Template J, clipping where necessary to keep the rounded shape. Pin this circle in position covering the raw edges of the petals. You may have to adjust the petals or the circle to get the proper arrangement. When you are pleased, applique the petals in position; then applique the circle as in **Fig 55**.

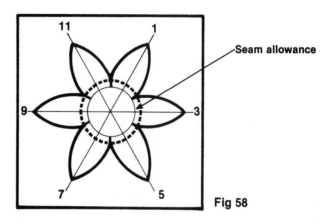

Fig 58

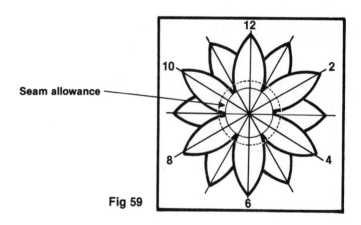

Fig 59

7. Remeasure the block and cut it so that it is exactly 8½″ × 8½″, keeping the center in its same position.

Cut the following pieces:

Template F	2 Fabric I
Template F	2 Fabric II
Template F	2 Fabric III
Template F	2 Fabric IV
Template F	2 Fabric V
Template F	2 Fabric VII
Template J	1 Fabric VIII
One 9″ × 9″ Square	Fabric VI

Enlarging the Sampler Quilt

After you have finished your sampler wall hanging, you may want to start on a larger quilt. The same general instructions apply no matter what size quilt you make. Simply construct more blocks. For a quilt large enough for a twin bed, make 35 blocks and set them five across and seven down **(Fig 60)**. For a double-bed sized quilt, make 42 blocks and set them six across and seven down **(Fig 61)**. You can repeat some of your favorite blocks two or three times; eliminate the ones that you detested making; make the quilt using all of the same blocks—you are now a quilt designer. The fabric requirements listed below are based upon a fairly even repetition of the twelve blocks.

TWIN BED

Fig 60

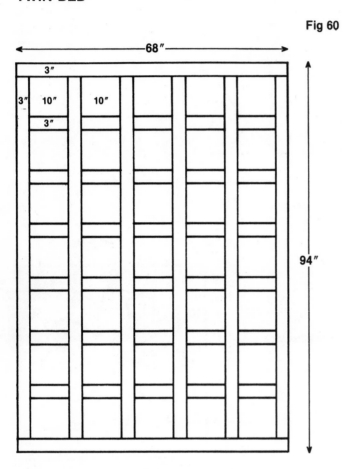

Add ½″ all around for binding

DOUBLE BED

Fig 61

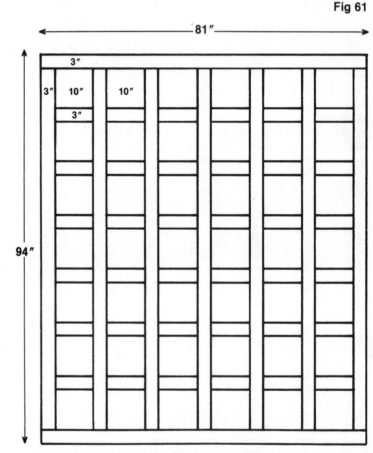

Add ½″ all around for binding

Fabric Requirements

¾ yard of each of the following prints: Fabric II, Fabric III, Fabric IV, Fabric V, Fabric VII (for patches and applique)

1 yard Fabric VI (for patches and background fabric for appliqued blocks)

3 yards Fabric I (for patches, sashing, borders and binding)

1⅓ yards Fabric IX (for framing)

4½ yards Fabric VIII (for one patch and backing)

Fabric Requirements

1 yard of each of the following prints: Fabric II, Fabric III, Fabric IV, Fabric V, Fabric VII (for patches and applique)

2 yards Fabric VI (for patches and background fabric for appliqued blocks)

5 yards Fabric I (for patches, sashing, borders and binding)

1¾ yards Fabric IX (for framing)

6 yards Fabric VIII (for one patch and backing)